T0349680

A HANDWRITTEN LEGACY

DAD'S STORY

A MEMORY AND KEEPSAKE
JOURNAL FOR MY FAMILY

Paige Tate & Co.

Dad's Story : A Memory and Keepsake Journal For My Family
Copyright © Korie Herold
Published in 2022 by Blue Star Press
Paige Tate & Co. is an imprint of Blue Star Press
PO Box 8835, Bend, OR 97708
contact@paigetate.com | www.paigetate.com

Illustrations and Design by Korie Herold

ISBN: 9781950968886
Printed in Colombia
10 9 8 7 6 5 4 3

This journal is dedicated to :

INTRODUCTION

This is the book I dream of handing every father as he enters into the sacred space of fatherhood.

Having children makes you begin to really reflect on your own life, and what you want to pass down and share with your children. Filling this in should feel like a few chapters in your life story, a story that is constantly evolving and growing into something else as time goes on.

One of my favorite experiences in life has been watching my husband, Joel, become a father. This book exists to honor this season in his life, and be able to share his thoughts with our sons. This book will be his written legacy, and I already can't wait to read it. I know it will be a treasure for my boys as well, as they grow up and learn more and more about their father.

This book is *your* written legacy.

I want your life story to live on in a meaningful way, which is why I created this keepsake book for you. My hope is that this will be a special space where you can dive into your story, pour out your heart, and pass your values and memories on to the people you love.

There are many ways you can record your story these days, but what I love about doing it in a physical book is that you get to write your memories by hand. I love handwriting—neat handwriting, messy handwriting, methodical handwriting, all of it. Handwriting is like a thumbprint that is unique to each person. I think personal storytelling is much more powerful when you get to read words that a person wrote down by hand. It means they were holding the book as they were writing in it. Their marks are now in your hands. I know you feel the difference, and I'm guessing that's why you selected this book.

A tip as you get started : Don't try to fill this book out all at once. Take your time and enjoy the process. Make yourself some tea or coffee, and settle in to tell your story on these pages. I can't stress enough that this process is meant to be enjoyed by you, the storyteller. If writing ever becomes overwhelming, simply set this book aside and come back to it later with fresh eyes. Your family will be forever grateful that you took the time to do this.

A note about *Dad's Story* : How you answer the questions may vary based on your age and amount of life lived when you start writing. It's important to note your age at the time of filling in this book, and it can be done on the book plate found inside the front cover. Also, if some of the questions don't apply to you, feel free to change the question or get creative in your response. You may not love every question, but imagine your child asking them of you and how you'd like to respond. These are for them after all, and kids want to know your story, even the hard parts.

So, go ahead. You have full permission to share your thoughts and story in a way only you can do. Get to it!

Onward and Upward,
Korie Herold

I would love to see *Dads Story* in your hands. Use #DadsStory and tag @korieherold to connect on social media.

EXPERIENCE IS
THE HARDEST
KIND OF TEACHER.
IT GIVES YOU
THE TEST FIRST
AND THE LESSON
AFTERWARD.

OSCAR WILDE

CHAPTER ONE

Early Childhood

MY FULL NAME : _____

_____

THE STORY BEHIND MY NAME : _____

_____

_____

_____

_____

_____

_____

_____

_____

_____

_____

MY NICKNAMES GROWING UP : _____

_____

_____

_____

_____

MY BIRTHDAY : _____

_____

WHERE I WAS BORN : _____

_____

_____

_____

_____

_____

HOW I'D DESCRIBE MY PARENTS :

WHAT MY PARENTS DID FOR A LIVING :

HOW I'D DESCRIBE MY GRANDPARENTS : _____

_____

_____

_____

_____

_____

_____

_____

_____

_____

_____

_____

_____

_____

_____

_____

_____

_____

WHAT MY GRANDPARENTS DID FOR A LIVING : _____

_____

_____

_____

_____

_____

HERE'S WHAT OUR HOUSE WAS LIKE GROWING UP :

MY RELATIONSHIP(S) WITH MY SIBLINGS/COUSINS :

THIS IS WHO I PLAYED WITH THE MOST GROWING UP : _____

MY FAVORITE TOYS OR PLAY-TIME ACTIVITIES : _____

HOW I'D DESCRIBE MY CHILDHOOD BEDROOM : _____

FAMILY MEALTIME AS A CHILD WAS LIKE THIS :

MY PETS GROWING UP :

MY FAVORITE EARLY CHILDHOOD MEMORY : _____

WHAT I MISS MOST ABOUT BEING A CHILD : _____

ADD PHOTO

ADDITIONAL THOUGHTS OR STORIES ABOUT MY EARLY CHILDHOOD :

CHAPTER TWO

The School Years

MY FRIENDS IN SCHOOL :

MY FAVORITE SCHOOL SUBJECT :

ACTIVITIES, SPORTS, OR CLUBS I WAS INVOLVED IN :

WHAT I ENJOYED DOING OUTSIDE OF SCHOOL :

MY FAVORITE MUSIC, TV SHOWS, AND BOOKS GROWING UP :

WHAT I THOUGHT I WANTED TO BE WHEN I GREW UP :

HOW I'D DESCRIBE MYSELF AS A TEENAGER :

WHERE I LIVED, AND WHAT SCHOOLS I ATTENDED :

A MEMORABLE TIME I GOT IN TROUBLE :

MY FAVORITE HIGH SCHOOL MEMORY :

MY FAVORITE TEACHER/COACH, AND WHAT MADE THEM SO GREAT :

MY FASHION/CLOTHING STYLE IN HIGH SCHOOL :

MY THOUGHTS/EXPERIENCE ON LEARNING HOW TO DRIVE :

WHAT I WOULD HAVE DONE DIFFERENTLY IN SCHOOL IF I HAD THE CHANCE :

WHAT I DID AFTER HIGH SCHOOL :

WHAT I MISS MOST ABOUT SCHOOL :

A MEMORABLE VACATION I WENT ON DURING MY SCHOOL YEARS :

ADD PHOTO

ADDITIONAL THOUGHTS OR STORIES ABOUT MY TIME IN SCHOOL :

CHAPTER THREE

Work & Travel

MY FIRST JOB : _____

_____

_____

_____

_____

_____

_____

_____

MY CURRENT JOB, AND WHAT I ENJOY ABOUT IT : _____

_____

_____

_____

_____

_____

_____

_____

_____

THE JOB THAT SHAPED ME THE MOST IN LIFE AND WHY : _____

_____

_____

_____

_____

_____

_____

_____

MY LONGEST HELD JOB WAS :

MY DREAM CAREER WOULD LOOK LIKE THIS :

MY THOUGHTS ON RETIREMENT :

ADVICE I'D SHARE ABOUT WORKING :

MY FIRST CAR :

THE CAR THAT CARRIES THE MOST SIGNIFICANT MEMORIES WITH IT, AND WHAT
THOSE ARE :

THE VEHICLE I HOPE TO DRIVE ONE DAY :

THE FAMILY VACATIONS I HOLD DEAREST :

THE FURTHEST PLACE I'VE TRAVELED UP UNTIL NOW :

MY FAVORITE PLACE TO TRAVEL :

WHERE I HOPE TO TRAVEL ONE DAY :

ADD PHOTO

ADDITIONAL THOUGHTS OR STORIES ABOUT WORK AND TRAVELING :

CHAPTER FOUR

Love & Family

MY FIRST DATE : _____

_____

_____

_____

_____

_____

_____

_____

_____

_____

_____

_____

THE STORY OF MY FIRST KISS : _____

_____

_____

_____

_____

_____

_____

_____

_____

_____

THE MOST ROMANTIC MOMENT OF MY LIFE :

HOW I MET YOUR MOTHER :

HOW LONG WE DATED BEFORE WE SETTLED DOWN :

A FAVORITE TIME OF MINE SPENT WITH YOUR MOTHER :

MY BEST RELATIONSHIP ADVICE :

HOW MY CHILDREN'S NAMES WERE CHOSEN : _____

_____

_____

_____

_____

_____

_____

_____

_____

HOW I'D DESCRIBE RAISING OUR FAMILY : _____

_____

_____

_____

_____

_____

_____

_____

_____

_____

_____

_____

_____

THE MEAL/DISH I MOST ENJOY SHARING WITH OUR FAMILY :

MY FAVORITE MEMORY OF RAISING OUR FAMILY :

WHAT I ENJOY MOST ABOUT HAVING YOUNG CHILDREN IN THE HOUSE :

HOW WE CELEBRATE BIRTHDAYS IN OUR HOME :

A FAVORITE BIRTHDAY OF MINE AND WHAT MADE IT SO MEMORABLE :

HOW I FELT THE DAY I FOUND OUT I WAS GOING TO BE A FATHER :

SOMETHING I FEEL LIKE I AM DOING WELL AS A FATHER :

SOMETHING I STRUGGLE WITH AS A FATHER :

MY DEFINITION OF THE WORD "LOVE" :

ADD PHOTO

ADDITIONAL THOUGHTS OR STORIES ABOUT FAMILY & RELATIONSHIPS : _____

CHAPTER FIVE

Character & Values

THREE CHARACTERISTICS ABOUT MYSELF THAT I VALUE : _____

_____

_____

_____

_____

_____

_____

HOW PEOPLE WHO KNOW ME WELL WOULD DESCRIBE ME : _____

_____

_____

_____

_____

_____

_____

THREE TRAITS I VALUE IN MY FRIENDS AND FAMILY, OR WHEN MAKING
NEW RELATIONSHIPS :

_____

_____

_____

_____

_____

_____

A COMPLIMENT SOMEONE GAVE ME THAT I WILL
NEVER FORGET:

THE BEST PIECE OF ADVICE I EVER RECEIVED :

UP TO THIS POINT, HERE'S THE ONE THING I WOULD HAVE DONE DIFFERENTLY WITH
OR IN MY LIFE :

UP TO THIS POINT, THIS IS THE MOST CHARACTER-DEFINING EVENT OF MY LIFE :

THE HARDEST THING I'VE EVER GONE THROUGH :

SOMETHING I WASN'T PREPARED FOR AS A PARENT :

ONE OF MY PROUDEST MOMENTS :

MY FAVORITE QUOTE OR VERSE THAT GUIDES ME :

THE ROLE OF FAITH OR SPIRITUALITY IN MY LIFE :

THE THINGS I VALUE MOST IN LIFE :

THE VALUES I HOPE TO PASS DOWN AND INSTILL IN MY FAMILY :

MY FAVORITE WAY TO MAKE OTHERS FEEL LOVED/SPECIAL :

ADD PHOTO

ADDITIONAL THOUGHTS ON CHARACTER AND VALUES :

CHAPTER SIX

Hypotheticals & Curiosities

IF I COULD THROW A DINNER PARTY AND INVITE 3 OTHER PEOPLE, DEAD OR ALIVE, THIS IS WHO I WOULD INVITE AND WHY :

ONE THING I WANT TO TRY OR EXPERIENCE :

ONE THING I THINK YOU SHOULD LEARN MORE ABOUT AND WHY IT'S WORTH IT :

MY GIFTS AND TALENTS, AND HOW I USE THEM IN MY LIFE :

THE BEST PURCHASE I'VE EVER MADE, AND WHAT MADE IT SO MEMORABLE :

SOMETHING I HOPE TO PURCHASE IN THE FUTURE, AND WHY :

BOOKS, MUSIC, ART, AND FILMS THAT I ENJOY :

IF I COULD HAVE A ROBOT TAKE OVER ONE CHORE FOR ME, IT WOULD BE THIS :

HOW I'D DESCRIBE THE PERFECT DAY IF IT WERE UP TO ME :

MY FAVORITE WAY TO TREAT MYSELF :

ONE THING ABOUT ME THAT MAY SURPRISE YOU :

SOUNDS THAT BRING ME JOY TO HEAR :

SIMPLE THINGS IN LIFE THAT BRING ME GREAT JOY :

MY FAVORITE GAME TO PLAY :

THE MOST INTERESTING PERSON I HAVE EVER MET :

THE PERSON THAT INSPIRES ME THE MOST :

THE NATIONAL OR WORLD EVENTS THAT I REMEMBER MOST FROM MY LIFETIME :

SOMETHING I'M REALLY BAD AT NO MATTER HOW HARD I TRY :

MY PET PEEVES :

THE THREE THINGS THAT I OWN THAT MEAN THE MOST TO ME :

ADD PHOTO

ADDITIONAL THOUGHTS I'D LIKE TO SHARE ABOUT MY LIFE :

CHAPTER SEVEN

Words of Wisdom

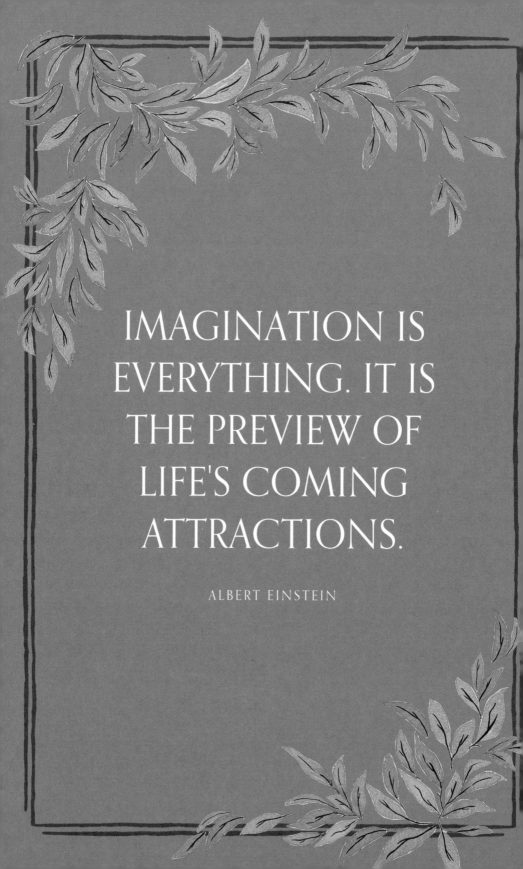

IMAGINATION IS
EVERYTHING. IT IS
THE PREVIEW OF
LIFE'S COMING
ATTRACTIONS.

ALBERT EINSTEIN

Words of Wisdom

This chapter of the book is open-ended and up to you as
to how you choose to use it. These pages can serve as a
continuation of the stories you tell from the previous sections
if you need more room to write. Additionally, it can serve
as a place to write letters and share words of wisdom you've
gained over the years. It's completely up to you.

Here are some suggestions to write about in this chapter :

ADVICE ABOUT FAITH

ADVICE ABOUT DATING

ADVICE ABOUT MARRIAGE

ADVICE ABOUT RAISING A FAMILY

ADVICE ABOUT FACING TRIALS

ADVICE ABOUT FORGIVENESS

ADVICE ABOUT MAKING BIG DECISIONS

STORIES ABOUT BEING A FATHER

A LETTER OF HOPE FOR MY CHILDREN'S FUTURE

YOUR STORIES ARE WORTH TELLING

We believe this in our core, which is why we're creating the heirloom books that we do. We believe in quality materials, timeless design, and a whole lot of heart. We invite you to visit our website to dive into any of the books in our current lineup and get a deeper look at the contents, purpose of the book, who it's for, and what makes each one special.

WWW.KORIEHEROLD.COM
for more information

OTHER BOOKS BY KORIE HEROLD

GROWING YOU : A KEEPSAKE PREGNANCY JOURNAL AND MEMORY BOOK FOR MOM & BABY - *Growing You* is an heirloom-quality book to celebrate and chronicle your pregnancy journey, reflecting on the growth, anticipation, and memories that you want to hold onto as a mother. This journal is the perfect gift for someone early on in their pregnancy.

AS YOU GROW : A MODERN MEMORY BOOK FOR BABY - *As You Grow* stands out from the crowd of baby books with its elegant, chic, and timeless design. The guided sections with gender-neutral artwork provide space for your family to record moments from pregnancy to age five. *As You Grow* is inclusive of every modern family and makes a great gift for a parent at a baby shower.

GROWING UP : A MODERN MEMORY BOOK FOR THE SCHOOL YEARS - *Growing Up* is a modern memory book for the school years and features gender-neutral artwork and space to record precious memories from kindergarten through high school so you can one day pass it down to your grown child.

OUR CHRISTMAS STORY : A MODERN MEMORY BOOK FOR CHRISTMAS - Write down meaningful holiday traditions, record special gifts given or received, save photos with Santa or annual family Christmas cards, preserve treasured family holiday recipes, and so much more! This book makes for a thoughtful gift for a bridal shower, wedding gift, or for a family who loves to celebrate Christmas.

AROUND OUR TABLE : A MODERN HEIRLOOM RECIPE BOOK TO ORGANIZE AND PRESERVE YOUR FAMILY'S MOST CHERISHED MEALS - Preserve all of your favorite recipes, and the memories associated with them, in this heirloom-quality blank recipe book that includes 7 sections to organize your recipes, along with recipe cards, plastic sleeves to preserve new and old recipes, and a pocket folder in the back for additional storage.

AS WE GROW : A MODERN MEMORY BOOK FOR MARRIED COUPLES - *As We Grow* is a place to celebrate and remember the details of your marriage. Record the story of how you live and love and preserve it in writing—a treasure you can pass to your children and grandchildren. It's the perfect gift for the newly engaged couple, the newly married couple, or those who have been married for years!

GRANDMA'S/GRANDPA'S STORY : A MEMORY AND KEEPSAKE JOURNAL FOR MY FAMILY - These two guided journals provide grandparents with thoughtful writing prompts to help them record their most precious moments and pass them down to their grandchildren and families. Beautifully designed keepsake journals, these books are the perfect gift for Mother's/Father's Day, birthdays, or any special occasion.

MORE THAN GRATITUDE - Spend 100 days cultivating deep roots of gratitude through guided journaling, prayer, and scripture. *More Than Gratitude* is ready to meet you where you are, and help you grow in your daily walk with the Lord, through six simple daily prompts. Grab your sisters, neighbors, friends, and family and do this journey together!

WHAT PEOPLE ARE SAYING
ABOUT KORIE HEROLD BOOKS

"Korie is an artist at heart but also has an overwhelming sense of legacy to everything she does. Her other books have a way of making you pause, slow down, and memorialize a fleeting season to enjoy later." - Lauren Swann

"When you see how beautiful and detail-oriented her books are, you become a customer for life. Thank you, Korie, for thinking of everything and creating treasures that will be passed down through future generations." - Paige Frey

"The quality is unbelievable and it's such a gorgeous place to preserve all those cherished memories. And it looks beautiful on my shelf next to my other memory books from Korie! ... I love the attention to detail Korie includes in her books." - Maria Hilsenbrand

"By far, I think my favorite thing about As You Grow *is that my son will one day be able to cherish this time capsule of sorts. He'll know exactly how he was loved, thought of, and remembered as my sweet little boy."* - Alyse Morrissey

WWW.KORIEHEROLD.COM